Motivation 101:

Ten Ways to Increase Your Daily Motivation

By

Paul G. Brodie

Motivation 101: Ten Ways to Increase Your Daily Motivation

Copyright @ 2015 by Paul G. Brodie

Editing by Devin Rene Hacker

Published in the United States by BrodieEDU Publishing, 2015.

Disclaimer

The following viewpoints in this book are those of Paul Brodie. These views are based on his personal experience over the past forty years on the planet Earth, especially while living in the great state of Texas.

The intention of this book is to share his stories of struggles with weight and what has worked for *him* through his journey. It is highly recommended that you consult with your doctor prior to any weight loss plan and potential lifestyle change.

The views expressed are based on his personal experiences within the corporate world, education, and everyday life.

This book is dedicated to my mom, Barbara "Mama" Brodie. Without her support and motivation (and incredible cooking) I would not be here today.

I am also dedicating this book to everyone who has had struggles in life, especially with weight. Our greatest battle will always be against ourselves, and winning that battle will be our greatest victory.

Contents

Foreword

It is a privilege to know Paul Brodie, both as my brother and also my friend. Paul and I grew up apart, and on different sides of the Atlantic. Meeting for the first time as young adults, from the outset as a man in his early 20's, he impressed me with his commitment to family (especially our mom,) his work ethic, and strong sense of social justice. As you will read in this book, over the years, Paul went from working in the corporate world to being an educator (something we share). He spent the time working out what truly motivated him in life and what he wanted his life to look like. Through hard work and determination Paul has achieved this, and I am delighted that he is now sharing with you the tools which made it happen.

Paul shares some of his life experiences with a disarming honesty. It is this quality in particular which makes him stand out as a motivational writer and speaker. He neither glosses over difficulties in his life, nor does he dwell on them. Paul is qualified to write about motivation because he has it – in spades – and lives every day authentically and with purpose. Like all of us, he has good days and bad days. Through understanding himself and what personally motivates himself, he is able to re-focus and work through difficulties using the motivational tools outlined in this book which he developed and lives by.

I value my relationship with Paul immensely. As his sister, I will say he is accurate (while sometimes annoyingly) about what is good for me, even though I may not always want to hear it. The most important advice can be the hardest to hear. Paul's skills as an honest yet empathic communicator makes him successful at convincingly getting his point across.

I will never forget the time when I was getting over the break-up with my partner, one of the most difficult times of my life, he encouraged me through the sadness to remember what my life purpose is, even though I was reluctant to hear it at the time. Paul's chapter **Our Greatest Opponent** was a reminder to me of how we are both our greatest motivator and our greatest opponent, often at the same time. His questions ending every chapter are designed to help us understand ourselves, our life motivation, and how we have to actively motivate ourselves every day.

Paul has a rare quality as a motivational speaker – he makes you feel like he is talking to you personally, even if there are 100 people in the room. This book gives you the opportunity to go on that personal journey with him as your companion. It will challenge you and make you laugh, (Paul's slightly offbeat humor is somewhat legendary in the family), but most of all I hope that it will encourage and motivate you to live your life authentically and with purpose every day.

Dr. Heather Ottaway
Bristol, UK.

Introduction

Our own motivation is what helps define our lives. In this book I will specifically cover ten major points of motivation that I utilize in my seminars. I created the Motivation 101 seminar in 2013, with the goal to help motivate people, and to also help my audience with finding their motivation in life. Each of the chapters covers one of ten ways in which we can increase our daily motivation. At the end of each chapter I ask several questions, that if answered honestly, I believe will help you to find personal motivation.

Chapter 1 begins with the first question you must ask yourself, what motivates you? What fires you up in life? What do you live for?

Chapter 2 is dedicated to how you start your day. Starting your day on the right note sets the tone for your day ahead. As a teacher, I must start the school day strong and I will share what I have done that has worked well for me.

Chapter 3 explores the power that music can have on your day. I cannot emphasize how important music is in your everyday life.

Chapter 4 is simple. Just Do It! You might have heard that slogan before, and we will cover just how important those three words can be.

Chapter 5 reveals our greatest opponent; sneak peak, it's ourselves!

Chapter 6 encourages you to find your purpose. We all have a purpose in life. Once you find your purpose you will know why you are here.

Chapter 7 is about environment. We are all a product of our environment. My philosophy is that the weaknesses of people allow them to become a part of any environment they are in. However, people who know their purpose and believe in themselves, will create their own environment.

Chapter 8 details how we are Masters of Our Universe. Here I will show you that the only perception that matters in your life is your own! Homage is also paid to the importance of friends and family in our pursuit to be the master of our own universe.

Chapter 9 is about forgiveness. Gandhi once said that "forgiveness is the attribute of the strong", and that is why it is critical to learn to forgive. Forgiveness is not for the person who has hurt you, but for ourselves.

Chapter 10 is dedicated to D.R.E.A.M. Do, Relevant, Enjoy, Aspire, and Meaning. In our final chapter I will cover how you can apply D.R.E.A.M to your personal motivation.

I hope that this book helps you in your journey to discover your own personal motivation. My philosophy in anything I do from teaching, to giving motivational seminars and writing, is to have the power of one. My goal is to help at least one person. I hope that person is you.

Chapter 1 - What Motivates You?

When I created my Motivation 101 seminar in 2013, the first set of questions that I asked my audience was what motivates you? What fires you up? What are you passionate about? I received a lot of different responses ranging from the start of a new day, accomplishing goals, skiing, family, music, pets, and cars. The second set of questions I asked is what do you *use* to get motivated? What do you *use* to make it through the day? The answers I typically get are music, coffee, soft drinks, and prayer.

The point of asking these questions was to get my audience to think of what is important to them and what motivates them. Once you know what motivates you then you can use those things in your everyday life.

Motivation is very personal and specific to each and every person. What motivates me is my family. My family and close friends are the most important things in my life and I truly feel that they contribute greatly to all of my success.

Making a difference is a motivator for me. It was one of the main motivators when I made the decision to leave the corporate world in 2007, and take a leap of faith entering the teaching profession. As an educator now for the past eight years, I have had the honor of making a difference in the lives of my kids and their parents. Nothing to me is more rewarding.

Once you know what motivates you in life, it will help clarify where you are, but more importantly, where you want to go.

Chapter 2 - Starting Your Day

Starting your day on the right note makes all the difference in your continued journey for personal motivation. I believe that the most important part of our day is the first hour that we are awake in the morning.

On school days I typically wake around 6:00 am. Since I usually get to bed around 11:00 pm, I am typically running on seven hours of sleep during the week. The first thing I do is take my thyroid pill, (my first book Eat Less and Move More explains why I am on a thyroid pill and also my career in education). I then grab my iPhone, and refer to a list I have saved of my morning motivations. Reading this helps me to get my mind centered and feeling positive to start the day. This morning motivation list is updated at least two to three times per month so that I am constantly adding things to motivate myself.

The list includes statements to get me focused such as:

What will happen in life will happen because my direction in life is already set.

Keep calm and let karma finish it.

I am going to win.

Only thing that matters is **YOUR** perception of **YOUR** life. No one else's opinion of you matters.

Only **YOUR** opinion is what is relevant in **YOUR** life.

You are the **MASTER** of your own **UNIVERSE**. Focus on how great your life is versus what you don't have.

The list also helps especially if I wake up feeling negative or if I had a nightmare. One of the worst feelings when getting up is waking up from a nightmare. I only have one fear in life and that is failure. Over the years I have learned to master most of my dreams where I will usually realize mid dream that it isn't real and that I can control the dream from that point. There are times that I do not though and the list really helps in those situations.

Once I read the list and get myself centered, I get a shower. That morning shower is key to waking up in the morning as feeling good makes a big difference in the morning process.

After getting a shower, and making sure I have waited the full thirty minutes after my thyroid pill, I have my first morning cappuccino, spend time with my mom, my cat and two dogs. Spending that family time in the morning to me makes all the difference.

By 6:50 am I am heading to work. My thirty minute commute from Arlington, TX to Bedford, TX is when the power of music makes all the difference in keeping the positive momentum going as my motivation for the day ahead.

Ask yourself the following questions. What is the first thing I do when I wake up? Do I typically feel positive or negative when I wake up? What is my morning ritual? Do I have a morning motivation list that I should read when I first wake up to get my mind centered? What do I listen to on the way to work?

Chapter 3 - Power of Music

The power of music makes all the difference to me with motivation throughout the day. I am very particular about the music I play on the way to work each morning. There are multiple playlists that I have for different moods. The most important part is that the music is motivating, has a great beat, and also gets the blood pumping.

During the spring of 2015, I found the Furious 7 soundtrack, and I played that soundtrack every morning for a month. Not only did the music pump me up and get me motivated for the day, but it also got me to work a little quicker as I felt part of the movie when I was driving (never forgetting that I was a law abiding citizen of the road, of course.) The Dark Knight Soundtrack was also a favorite.

I am also a huge believer in having a dance party in your car when you are driving. During my first year of teaching, one of my favorite songs was "Let It Rock" by Kevin Rudolf. I would hear the first part of the song and suddenly my right shoulder would move with the beat. A moment later my left shoulder would join the party. Thirty seconds later I was dancing in my car. I felt great.

As a teacher, I am a firm believer in music playing throughout my classes during the day. I believe it benefits not only the students, but also the teacher and classroom environment. My students are usually seventh through ninth grade and between the ages twelve to sixteen years old. Kids in that age can have a wide variety of emotions from minute to minute. Getting their attention through music is a wonderful tool to inspire learning. Not only can they enjoy the beats of Michael Jackson, or lulling of the Beatles, but I can help make a difference in their moods, liven the classroom, and expose them to the music of history.

Early in the morning, the kids tend to be sleepy and at times rather grumpy. Music has served as a great equalizer in waking up and motivating my kids. We have a deal that as long as they are working on their assignment and following the rules, then I would always play music. It serves as a great classroom management tool and also a reward for good behavior.

One of the best examples over the past year was when I played "Happy" by Pharrell Williams. Within one minute my class was awake and ready to go. I would also make that the first song played when we did group activities that involved team work and movement. The kids would move around to match science and English vocabulary on word walls, do vocabulary drills and review, and even have a little dance party, which put smiles on all of our faces.

My afternoon class was, in all honesty, my favorite class. One of our rituals was to listen to "What Is Love" by Haddaway. The song was a hit in the early nineties and then had a revival with the movie "A Night at the Roxbury." The movie is based on two characters from Saturday Night Live who bobbed their heads to the left if that song came on, no matter where they were. That's what I wanted for my kids. To be able to stop, and enjoy the music.

Music is a huge part in successfully motivating workouts. I have specific mixes that I detailed in *Eat Less and Move More*, such as, "Till I Collapse" by Eminem, "Eye of the Tiger" by Survivor, and "The Champ is here" by Jadakiss.

For my summer mix in 2015, I chose boxing movie themes. Movies like Rocky always focused on a boxing as the metaphor for the battle against ourselves, which is our greatest battle in life.

Below is the second summer mix that I made. It was successful in keeping me motivated. I hope it will help you too.

Brodie's Second Thirty Minute Workout Mix 2015

1. Rocky Theme Song
2. Rocky Training Montage
3. "Turn Down for What" by DJ Snake and Lil Jon
4. "Phenomenal" by Eminem
5. Conor McGregor Entrance Music Foggy Dew - Hypnotize
6. "The Champ Is Here" by Jadakiss
7. "Eye of the Tiger" by Survivor
8. Going the Distance
9. Bad Blood by Taylor Swift

Think about how you feel when you hear the theme from Rocky. It pumps me up every time I have ever heard the song. It is always the first song I play when working out to set the tone.

Ask yourself the following questions. What type of music do I listen to on the way to work? Do I have song mixes for different moods? Should I make a workout mix to help motivate myself to work out?

Chapter 4 - Just Do It

In early July 2015, I was still deciding when I should start writing my book *Eat Less and Move More*. I was originally going to wait until I hit my goal weight of 250 pounds. When that didn't happen, and for two additional years, I put off writing the book. I was on a flight to Las Vegas and I decided that it was time to not only write *Eat Less and Move More* but also write books based on my seminars.

Then I had a revelation. Why don't I write a brutally honest book about my weight loss and transformation? Not only will I write about the success but also about all of the personal struggles with gaining part of the weight back and then taking most of it off again. So many books are about how a certain diet changed someone's life and how everything seems just perfect. What isn't covered is falling down and more importantly what do you do when you fall.

We fall down, to paraphrase *The Dark Knight Trilogy,* so that we can get back up. I chose to get up and keep moving. I kept getting up and kept moving and that was the story that I wanted to share. I also decided to make it a two book series and that I would publish the second book when I hit the 250 pounds (thirty seven pounds to go) in the future.

Now that I was getting ready to write the book, I figured that I would get started in mid to late July and then I saw this crazy video by Shia LaBouef on YouTube that was probably one of the craziest videos that I have ever seen. Shia is a unique personality to say the least, but his message really resonated with me. I decided that it was time to Just Do It!

"Action is a high road to self-confidence and esteem. Where it is open, all energies flow toward it. It comes readily to most people and its rewards are tangible. The cultivation of the spirit is elusive and difficult and the tendency toward it is rarely spontaneous, whereas, the opportunities for action are many." Bruce Lee

Action was what I needed to do. I needed to Just Do It. It was time to write my first book.

From July 3-5, 2015 I wrote my entire first book *Eat Less and Move More.* I just did it by creating a word file and I started writing. After five hours of writing I had ten chapters and over 7000 words written. I just did it!

After day two and another four hours, I had seventeen chapters and just under 12,000 words. By the end of day three I had twenty one chapters and over 17,000 words.

Day four was dedicated to revisions and my word count grew over 18,000 words, my book, with the exception of edits was written. A project four years in the making was completed in three days. Just Do It!

The same thing applies to your motivation. Just Do It! In life we tend to overthink things. We will wait until we think things are going to be just right. In my situation I was going to put off writing the book until I hit the 250 pound mark. Instead I could now share my success and struggles regardless if I hit a number on a scale for the first book.

I also decided to apply the principle to when I need to work out. During the summer my goal is to work out three days a week. During summer 2015, my weight was back to where it needed to be after getting a little out of control. One of the main motivators to get in that pool is to just do it.

Half of the battle with working out in my view is just getting your workout clothes on. Then it is time to get your music together, go outside, and go to work. I made myself get into that pool even when I didn't feel like it and I always felt better once I got in the pool and got to work.

Ask yourself the following questions. What is holding me back? What is stopping me from just doing it? What am I waiting for? Have I watched the Shia LaBouef video on YouTube? When am I going to work out next?

Chapter 5 - Our Greatest Opponent

Our greatest opponent is a familiar one. It is the person that we see every day in the mirror. The greatest battle in life is not against another person, it is against ourselves. We are the greatest motivator and biggest obstacle to our successes in life. You also have a choice. Will you be your greatest champion or your worst enemy?

I remember the old looney tunes cartoons growing up where you see the cartoon character struggling to make a choice. The character, usually Sylvester the cat, would have the good version of him whispering in his ear on the right side, and his bad side whispering in his left side. He would listen to both sides of himself and would constantly struggle between which decisions to make.

I feel that many of us go through that same struggle daily. We all have good days and bad. One day we may feel like we are invincible and another day we might feel like we cannot accomplish anything and are depressed.

One of my greatest personal battles in my life has been depression. Most days I would feel great, but there are days when I feel depressed and question many things about my life. Depression is on both sides of my family and I have lost family members to depression over the years. It is also why I fight the battle to stay positive and to stay motivated on a daily basis.

Staying motivated and positive is something that is deeply personal to me. In chapter 2 I spoke about starting your day and wrote about the techniques that I use. I highly recommend that you also create a list of ways to motivate yourself, especially on those bad days. My morning motivation list really helps me when the depression strikes because I have trained myself to look at that list to remind myself how great life truly is.

Whether you believe in Astrology or not, I believe it's just another part of what explains why we are the way we are. As a Gemini, who are known to have two sides, can say I definitely have both. At times I am very social and at other times I just want to be by myself. I am as much as an extrovert who loves having a good time to an introvert who likes to spend time at home and read and relax.

Giving a seminar and teaching are great example of both my sides. I love to give seminars and teach but they take a lot out of my physically and emotionally. After the end of my seminars, I will typically go back to my hotel room or waiting area and just unwind and relax. During that time, I usually like to be by myself as I have had a lot of social stimulation.

The same thing happens after a day of teaching classes. By the time I get home all I want to do is unwind by watching sports center or reading for a little while as I have been around my kids all day. Eight hours of teaching including a balance of instruction and classroom management can wear out the best of teachers. Having that break once I get home is critical for my introvert side.

That is why we need to know ourselves in our greatest battle. If we can know and understand ourselves and our different sides then we can get through the day and also understand when we need a break. By understanding when we need to unwind, we can recharge and be ready to take on whatever life has in store for us. We will all have good days and challenging days.

Nothing in life is easy. Life will knock you on your butt at times. The question is, what you will do when you are down? I choose to rise and get up! My decision, similar to what Rocky said in Rocky Balboa, was to get up and keep moving. To get hit and keep moving because that is how winning is done in life.

Our character is not defined in the good times, but in the hard times. I got to know more about myself and what I could endure in my life when I was getting bullied and beaten up in the sixth grade. I could have given up and skipped school, instead I went to school every day and I fought back. Unfortunately as one person against a whole group, the fight is not always a fair one. I had many situations when I was against five to six kids and those odds are pretty tough to beat.

In Japan, athletes are not judged for just great athletic feats but especially for fighting spirit. Fighting spirit is the ability to get up again and again, to keep fighting to your best ability regardless whether you win or lose. We all have that fighting spirit in us and can overcome any and all odds, but only if we win the battle against ourselves and our own perception of our lives.

What I have learned in life is that the only perception that matters is our own. What we think of our own life is all that matters in my view. No one else's perception matters. When you realize about our own perception then you are on the way to winning the greatest battle in life. The battle against ourselves.

Ask yourself the following questions. Do I listen to my good or bad side more? What do I struggle with on a daily basis? What should I do to fight negativity? Am I an extrovert, introvert, or both?

Chapter 6 Find Your Purpose

In chapter one we covered what motivates you. In connection to our motivation we also need to find our purpose. To find your purpose you need to find out," What makes you happy?"

When I left the corporate world in 2007 I was not happy; I felt like a mercenary. In my book *Eat Less and Move More*, I talked about how I spent October to December finding what I wanted to do the rest of my career and finding my purpose.

During that time, I wrote out multiple lists about where my next step would be. Money was not that important as long as I had enough to pay the bills with a little left over at the end of the month. I wanted to have the opportunity to help others again.

My first post college job in 2005 was at Enterprise Rent-A-Car. I started as a Management Trainee, became a Management Assistant, and then an Assistant Manager. During that time I was able to help out a lot of up and coming employees by serving as a mentor in the mentoring program and training employees, which I loved doing.

I wanted to have a position after leaving the corporate world which would give me a little more time off. From 2005 to 2007, I had worked between 45-60 hours per week, and only taking one to two weeks off per year. Work/life balance had to be a huge factor in my next career step. I also wanted a position where I would be moving around, to support my healthy lifestyle. What I realized is that everything that I wanted was in education.

Mr. Brodie, Teacher. I had to think long and hard about that title. Could Paul Brodie, class clown, rebel, smart, but stubborn student, teach other students?

On February 14, 2008 I found the answer to that question and also found my purpose. I took my first assignment that day as a substitute teacher and would know very quickly if I either made the best or worst decision of my career.

I accepted an assignment to teach choir at a Junior High School in Arlington, TX, the same school district that I attended. What I would realize in the first fifteen minutes, is that this was either a horrible mistake or the greatest decision in my life. No pressure!

What could go wrong? Why wouldn't you want to spend a day teaching teenagers on Valentine's

Day? Actually, the day went well and I ended up falling in love with teaching within a few minutes after starting. I realized this was what I wanted to do in life and continued the process of getting certified as a teacher.

Mark Twain once said "The two most important days in your life are the day you are born … and the day you find out why." Valentine's Day 2008 will always stand out as that was the day that I found my purpose, and also the day I found out why I was born. I was born to be an educator and help others.

I always felt that I was going to make a difference in the lives of others, but actually knowing that my future was in teaching was a very powerful one. My two classrooms are my own classroom where I teach my kids, and at conferences and universities across the United States where I have given many motivational seminars. I knew that once I found my purpose, I would have my path for the rest of my career.

I also have the philosophy of The Power of One. If I have made a difference in at least one person's life through teaching, seminars, and my books, then I have achieved my main goal. In my view, money is not that important. Your quality of life and having a proper work life balance is what should matter the most. I made a lot of money in various jobs, I needed something more and decided to find my purpose.

My advice is not to follow the money. I was raised in an affluent household, when I was younger my family also lost everything. When my parents got divorced we ended up with nothing. My Mom didn't even have a car during my years in junior high and high school. I mention this because money never made me happy. Things are nice to have, but they don't bring happiness. Being obsessed with making money was not where I wanted to go in life. My goal was to make enough money to take care of the bills and to not live day-to-day. I have never bought a new car. My current car is my dream car, a 2009 Nissan Murano, which I love.

The road to happiness involves family and friends, and as long as you make enough money to cover the bills and have a little over, then that's all that matters in life. It is about who you spend your time with and how they make you feel. Thanks to all my family and friends, I feel like the richest man alive.

To find your purpose I suggest that you make a list that shows all of the things that you love to do. The questions that I have provided at the end of each chapter should help you realize what you love in life. Figure out where you want to work, my list included things like location (to save on time and gas), time off (plenty of time off for holidays and time off in the summer), helping people (working with kids), making a decent wage.

I've been presenting seminars since 2005, and noticed the connection between seminars and teaching. In 2005, I also started volunteering at the Special Olympics and loved working with the kids. It also helped guide me in a new direction in 2014 when I returned to the classroom as a Special Education Teacher.

One of the main things about finding your purpose is that we see the big picture in life. Life is more than just running errands, paying bills, making sure you have money, and making it through the day. Life is about giving back, helping people, and making a difference in the lives of others. Everything in life is about balance and finding your purpose will help you find that balance in life.

Morrie Schwartz once said that we should devote ourselves to creating things in life that gives us purpose and meaning. I feel that we are truly lost if we do not have purpose and meaning.

Think about organizations that you may have worked with in the past. Did you enjoy it? Would that be something you would be interested in pursuing as a career?

I am confident that through research, reflection and list writing that you too will eventually find your purpose if you have not already done so.

Ask yourself the following questions. What makes you happy? Have I evaluated what I want to do in life? Do I love what I am doing for my career? If I do not love what I am doing then why do I continue to do so? Is it because the money is too good to pass up?

Chapter 7 - Environment

We are all a product of our environment. My philosophy is that there are people that become a part of any environment they are in. However, strong people who know their purpose, and believe in themselves, will create their own environment. Morrie Schwartz said that you have to be strong enough to create your own culture if the culture around you does not work. This has been proven many times throughout my career.

In 2006, I was an assistant manager at Enterprise-Rent-A-Car. The branch location I was at was in Fort Worth, TX. We were in a great location. In addition to our main branch we also had Caliber Car Collision and Carswell Air Force Base.

When I started at that location we had a rotation of employees who would divide their time between the main branch and Caliber. Caliber was known for having a negative environment. So whenever rotations came around no one wanted to work there.

I found out that the general manager at Caliber hated our branch but I did not know why. That same day I went to visit the GM to ask what the issue was. He was direct and said that Enterprise by not having cars ready for their customers frustrated him. I took control, and told him that the buck stops here with me and that it is my responsibility to take care of the deals from now. I gave him my personal cell phone number and told him to call me anytime. Within the next month all of the employees loved working at Calber.

Three months later there was a huge summit between all of the Caliber and Enterprise leadership. Everyone was nervous. My area manager was especially nervous as the GM from my Caliber location was the first one to speak.

The first words out of his mouth were, "Paul Brodie gets it". He continued to talk about the rebuilding of the relationship between Enterprise and Caliber and how it is his goal to have all locations have the same positive relationship.

My classrooms over the years were also a product of environment. I made my classrooms as engaging and warm as possible for my kids and myself. Spending eight to nine hours in that room every day, I wanted it to be a place I would enjoy spending my day. My classrooms are always filled with posters which covered the subject matter, art that my kids made over the years, large flags of my favorite sports teams including the Dallas

Cowboys, Manchester United Soccer, and the Texas Longhorns. I also had copies of both my bachelors and master's degrees to show the importance of Education. I also had my high school diploma in my ESL classroom as I wanted my kids to constantly see the goals that were in sight for them.

The environment is not only the decorations or music that is played, but how you make people feel. Every place that I have worked, I made it my priority for that office, classroom, cubicle, and work area to be a happy environment.

An environment is what you make of it. Strong people create their own environment and I know that you can create any environment that you choose.

Ask yourself the following questions. Do I work in a positive environment? Have I ever changed my environment for the better? Am I the product of my environment? Have I ever created my own environment?

Chapter 8 - Master of Your Own Universe

We are all the master of our own universe. Our universe is our perception of how we view our lives. It is the only perception that matters. As I covered in chapter 2, I have a list that I read each morning about how I view things to get centered. One of the main things that I read each morning is that you are the MASTER of your own UNIVERSE.

Being the master of your own universe is simple. It is the belief that you control everything in your mind and thus everything in your world. Your emotions, thoughts, perceptions are all part of your own universe that you must master.

Every summer I have a number of books that I read. Summer 2015 found each book had a recurring theme, and that was the inner battle of ourselves to be a master of our own universe. It also showed how the writers, such as Bruce Lee, Ronda Rousey, and Mitch Albom, became masters of their own universes through their own perceptions and philosophies about their lives. All three overcame the odds in life.

Bruce Lee became one of the greatest martial artists ever. In *"The Tao of Jeet Kung Do"* he shares not only many martial arts techniques but also many of his philosophies about life. One of my favorite Bruce Lee quotes is from this book; "Relationship is understanding. It is a process of self-revelation. Relationship is the mirror in which you discover yourself -- to be is to be related." Relationships and understanding within ourselves is critical to becoming a master of our own universe.

Ronda Rousey shared in her book her philosophy on fighting and fighting ourselves "I learned how to fight and how to win. Whatever your obstacles, who-ever or whatever your adversary, there is a way to victory." I agree.

It is going to be a daily battle but take every day in stride. One of my favorite quotes is "Every day, in every way, I'm getting better and better." Emile Coue. I have always loved that quote because it is the simplest of truths.

Mitch Albom became a master of his own universe by reconnecting with his college professor Morrie Schwartz. Morrie was dying of ALS, Lou Gehrig's disease, and they would meet on Tuesday's to discuss life. Mitch, through this time, realized what was important in life, and through his time with Morrie, made his friends and family his priority instead of just his career,.

One of the greatest lessons from Tuesday's with Morrie was about love. "Invest in the human family. Invest in people. Build a little community of those you love and who love you." Morrie Schwartz.

Family and friends in my view critical to becoming a master of your own universe. The Beatles said it best that all you need is love. Love of family and close friends that become extended family are critical for our lives.

I am blessed to have an amazing group of family, and close friends that are my extended family. With their love and support, and successfully battling my inner demons, I have been able to become a master of my own universe.

Ask yourself the following questions. Do I believe that I control everything in my mind and thus everything in my world? Am I the master of my own universe? How important are my family and friends in my life?

Chapter 9 - Forgiveness

You must learn to forgive everyone who has ever hurt you to move on in your life. One of my favorite quotes from Mahatma Gandhi is:

"The weak can never forgive. Forgiveness is the act of the strong."

In my life I have been hurt by many people. I am sure you have been hurt as well. Hurt can turn to anger, anger to rage, and good people can go bad very quickly if lead on this destructive path. Now think about when you have forgiven someone who has hurt you.

Did you feel better?

Did you feel relieved?

I felt as if a huge weight has left my shoulders each time that I have forgiven someone.

My philosophy in life is to never purposely hurt anyone and to help as many people as possible. I was also severely bullied in the sixth grade. Every day for about five months I was covered in bruises from been punched throughout the day. No one did anything about it to help me. The situation got so bad that my mom had to move us out of the area. I could have held a grudge and hated those kids for the rest of my life, but I didn't. Within a few years I forgave every one of those kids.

Grudges are just not worth it. Ironically I ran into one of the kids when I was in my early twenties at a movie theater and he apologized about what happened and also how many of the other kids were sorry. I shook his hand and moved on.

One of my favorite quotes about forgiveness is "Accept the past as past, without denying it or discarding it." Morrie Schwartz. We must accept what has happened in our past and learn from it. We must forgive others to move on in our lives.

My classroom has served as a safe zone for many kids over the years and any bullying issues were resolved quickly. My kids always know that I have their backs and will always protect them. It is one of my proudest accomplishments as a teacher.

Ask yourself the following questions. Can I forgive someone who has hurt me? Have I ever forgiven someone? Did I feel better? Did I feel relieved?

Chapter 10 - D.R.E.A.M.

D.R.E.A.M. is an acronym that I created that stands for Do, Relevant, Enjoy, Aspire, and Meaning. I feel that if we can accomplish all aspects of D.R.E.A.M. then we are accomplishing what we want to do in life. When I accomplished D.R.E.A.M. I felt like my life is going in an amazing direction. Making a difference and helping others in life is something that I am very proud of and was a huge part of my D.R.E.A.M.

Do is simple. I refer to do as Just Do It. Don't think about it, don't put it off, and don't procrastinate. No excuses. Just Do It!

Make it Relevant. Make sure you feel that it is relevant to you. Make sure it is something important that you want to pursue in life. If it is not relevant to you then it will not be something that you care about.

Enjoy yourself! When you are doing something that you enjoy, it doesn't feel like work. Teaching and doing seminars are my fun, like having a louder conversation with a good friend. Find something that you love to do in life and see if you can potentially make a living doing it. Aspire for greatness. Find something that you want to aspire to. I aspired to be a teacher, motivational speaker, and author. Through years of following that dream I accomplished my goals. W. Clement Stone said "What the mind of Man can conceive and believe, it will achieve." I have always believed in that quote because as the master of our own universe, we can achieve anything that we set our minds to.

I was a B and C student in high school. My focus was on less challenging classes and I focused on fine arts with band, choir, and drama. My high school counselor during my senior year told my mom that my grades would not be good enough for a four year college and that I should consider junior college. I respectfully disagreed. Three months later I had a vocal scholarship from UT Arlington along with an acceptance letter from the university.

It took me ten long years to get my degree with working full time but I got my bachelor's degree in business management. Five years later I was graduating again with a Master of Arts degree in Teaching. I am convinced that we can do anything that we set our minds to. The only person who is stopping you, is you. Remember that our greatest battle with always be against ourselves.

The final part of D.R.E.A.M. is meaning. Find something meaningful in life to do. For me it was teaching, motivational speaking, and writing. It was also volunteering with the Special Olympics. If you ever want to see pure victory then I highly recommend going to the Special Olympics and watch those awesome kids compete in events.

I have volunteered in many roles with the Special Olympics and over the past ten years and I have had the opportunity to serve as the announcer for the medal ceremony in the gymnastics events. Seeing those kids' faces when I announce them as medalists is one of the greatest things you will ever see. The kids have such pride in their accomplishments, and their parents have so much love and pride for their kids. It is probably one of the most meaningful things I get to do outside teaching and highly recommend volunteering if you are not already doing so with an organization that you care about.

Ask yourself the following questions. Has someone ever told me that I cannot do something? What did I do?

What will I do to accomplish my D.R.E.A.M.?

Do

Relevant

Enjoy

Aspire

Meaning

Conclusion

I want to thank you for reading my second book. Writing these books are a labor of love for me. I write about things that I am passionate about and motivation is one of the most important things in life.

Through the past ten chapters we have covered a range of subjects from starting your day, the power of music, to forgiveness. What I hope is that this book has helped with your own personal motivation and that you will find your purpose and become the master of your own universe. When you do, you will feel truly free.

Free is when you don't care about the perception of others. Free is when you are pursuing your dreams. Free is when you're done putting things off and Just Do It! Free is knowing your purpose. Freedom is a beautiful thing and especially freedom from the perception of others. Free your mind and become your greatest champion.

About the Author

Paul Brodie is the President of BrodieEDU, an education consulting firm that specializes in the development of literacy programs, motivational seminars for universities and corporations, and wellness education. Brodie also serves as a Special Education Teacher for the Hurst-Euless-Bedford Independent School District.

From 2011-2014, Brodie served as a Grant Coordinator for the ASPIRE program in the

Birdville Independent School District. As coordinator, he created instructional and enrichment programming for over 800 students and 100 parents in the ASPIRE before and after school programs. He has also served for many years on the Board of Directors for the Leadership Development Council, Inc with leading the implementation of educational programming in low cost housing.

Previously, Brodie spent many years in the corporate world and decided to leave a lucrative career in the medical field to follow his passion and transitioned into education. From 2008 to 2011, he was a highly successful teacher in Arlington, TX where he taught English as a Second Language. Brodie turned a once struggling ESLprogram into one of the top programs in the school district. Many of his students have moved on to journalism, AVID, art classes, and a number of the students exited the ESL program entirely. His methods included music, movies, graphic novels, and many high engagement methods including using technology, games, cultural celebrations, and getting parents involved in their children's education. Brodie's approach has been called unconventional but highly effective, revolutionary, and highly engaging.
Brodie earned an M.A. in Teaching from Louisiana

College and B.B.A. in Management from the University of Texas at Arlington. He recently completed his first book: Eat Less and Move More: My Journey. Brodie hopes the book will help those like himself that have had challenges with weight and the goal of the book is to promote not only weight loss but also health and wellness.

His motivational seminars have been featured at multiple universities and at leadership conferences across the United States since 2005. Brodie is active in professional organizations and within the community and currently serves on the Advisory Board for Advent Urban Youth Development and as a volunteer with the Special Olympics. He continues to be involved with The International Business Fraternity of Delta Sigma Pi, and has served in many positions since 2002 including National Vice President – Organizational Development, Leadership Foundation Trustee, National Organizational Development Chair, District Director, and in many other volunteer leadership roles. He resides in Arlington, TX.

Acknowledgments

Thank you to God for guidance and protection throughout my life.

Thank YOU the reader for investing your time reading this book.

Thank you to my amazing mom, Barbara Brodie for all of the years of support and a kick in the butt when needed.

Thank you to my awesome sister, Dr. Heather Ottaway for writing my foreword and for all of the help and feedback with not only my book but also with my motivational seminars. It is scary how similar we are.

Thank you to Devin Hacker for serving as the editor of my second book. The slicing and dicing was very much appreciated and I could not have gotten this book published without her assistance.

Thank you to Lindsay Palmer who is working tirelessly to get me booked on college campuses for seminars throughout the United States. I could not have a better team of people to work with on Team Brodie.

Thank you to all who have served on the BrodieEDU Advisory Board.

Thank you to my dad, Bill "The Wild Scotsman" Brodie for his encouragement and support with the startup process of my books.

Thank you to Shannon and Robert Winckel (two members of the four horsemen with myself and our good friend, Derrada Rubell-Asbell) for their friendship and support. Shannon and Robert are two of my best teacher friends and are always great sounding boards for ideas.

Thank you to (Don) Omar Sandoval for his friendship and help with several BrodieEDU projects including building our awesome website.

Thank you to all of the amazing friends that I have worked with over the past twenty plus years. Each of them has made a great impact on my life.

Thank you to all of my students that I have had the honor to teach over the years. I am very proud of each of my kids.

Thank you to Delta Sigma Pi Business Fraternity. I learned a great deal about public speaking and leadership through the organization and every experience that I have had helped me become the person that I am today.

Thank you to my three best friends: J. Dean Craig, Jen Moorman, and Aaron Krzycki. We have gone through a lot together and I look forward to many more years of friendship.

Thank you to all of the students past and present at the UT Arlington and UT Austin chapters of DSP. Both schools mean a lot to me and I look forward to seeing them again at some point in the near future.

Thank you to the Lott Family (Stacy, Kerry, Lexi, and Austin) for their friendship over the past six years.

Thank you to Robin Clites for always taking care of things at the house with ensuring that Mom and I can always get that family vacation every year.

Contact Information

Interested in booking Paul for seminars, coaching, or consulting?

Testimonials from Paul's seminar attendees are available at www.BrodieEDU.com/testimonials

Paul can be reached at Brodie@BrodieEDU.com

Website www.BrodieEDU.com

@BrodieEDU on Twitter

BrodieEDU Facebook Page www.Facebook.com/BrodieEDU

BrodieEDU YouTube Channel www.YouTube.com/BrodieEDU

Feedback

Please leave a review for my book as I would greatly appreciate your feedback.

I also welcome you to contact me with any suggestions at Brodie@BrodieEDU.com

Special Offer

Are you a fan of audiobooks? I would like to offer you the audiobook of Motivation 101 for free. All you need to do is go to my website at www.BrodieEDU.com/freeaudiobook and provide your e mail address in exchange for the free digital download. The audiobook will only be available on the website for a limited time as I offer free goodies to my readership on a regular basis.